HEAR WHAT'S HERE

written by **MIKE AGRELIUS**

illustrated by **VAL CHADWICK BAGLEY**

Happy Valley Publishers

This book contains just a few words that sound the same,
aren't spelled the same, and have different meanings.
We know you can think of lots more. These words are called homophones.
Have fun learning and sharing what you've learned with others.

Mike and Val talked about doing this book for years. They finally did it.

This book would not have happened without help/encouragement from the following: Ruth, Carlyle, Doris, K2, Rod, Ray, K1, Tom, Donna, Cam, Dustin, Rachie, Jenners, Steve, Sums, and other Kickstarter supporters (especially Jason and Wendi).

Special mentions: Baylee, Tate, Jude, Dax, Nico, Bella, Maddy, Sabrina, Penny, Eva, Landyn, Rose, Louna, Kent, and Best Buddies.

Book layout and cover design by Kaitlin Barwick. Printed in China.

Happy Valley Publishers: Making quality, fun children's picture books and getting them into schools, libraries, and bookstores everywhere English is spoken (and some places where it isn't).

ISBN 978-0-936805-02-3

DEDICATED TO

Kids who like to learn stuff;
teachers who like to teach and put color in the gray matter;
parents, grandparents, and others who like to read with kids;
and anyone who thinks the English language is just a little whacky.

—M.G.A. AND V.C.B.

PAIR: Two; a couple; a set of two.

PEARS: Sweet fruit, smaller at the top and bigger at the bottom.

Do you SEE the SEA?

SEE: View; look; observe.

SEA: Body of water, usually larger than a lake, smaller than an ocean; often an extension of an ocean.

STARE: Look intently.   **STAIRS:** Set of steps, usually inside a home or building.

Would you
like to

STARE at
STAIRS?

Or maybe **BE a BEE?**

Boo

BE: Short for become; exist; allow.

BEE: A flighty insect with stinger, pollinates flowers, makes honey.

DEER: Swift footed, seemingly shy animal, often found in wooded areas.

DEAR: Much loved; precious.

NOT: Word that means no; negative.

KNOT: Fastening together of cords or strings as in ropes or shoes.

Is this **NOT** a **KNOT?**

Tell me what you **HEAR HERE.**

HEAR: Listen to.

HERE: In or at this place, now.

Last **NIGHT** the **KNIGHT** got caught.

NIGHT: Time from sunset to sunrise; darkness.

KNIGHT: Male recognized by monarchy for service, good deeds and/or valor.

WHALE: Large mammal that lives in water, has blow hole and tail.

WAIL: Loud, mournful cry.

Have you heard a WHALE WAIL?

HARE: An animal very much like a rabbit, slightly larger, with long ears and long hind legs.

HAIR: A fine, threadlike growth found on the head and skin of people and animals.

Or seen a **HARE** with **HAIR?**

Do you think this **PAIL** is **PALE?**

PAIL: Bucket.

PALE: Lacking color.

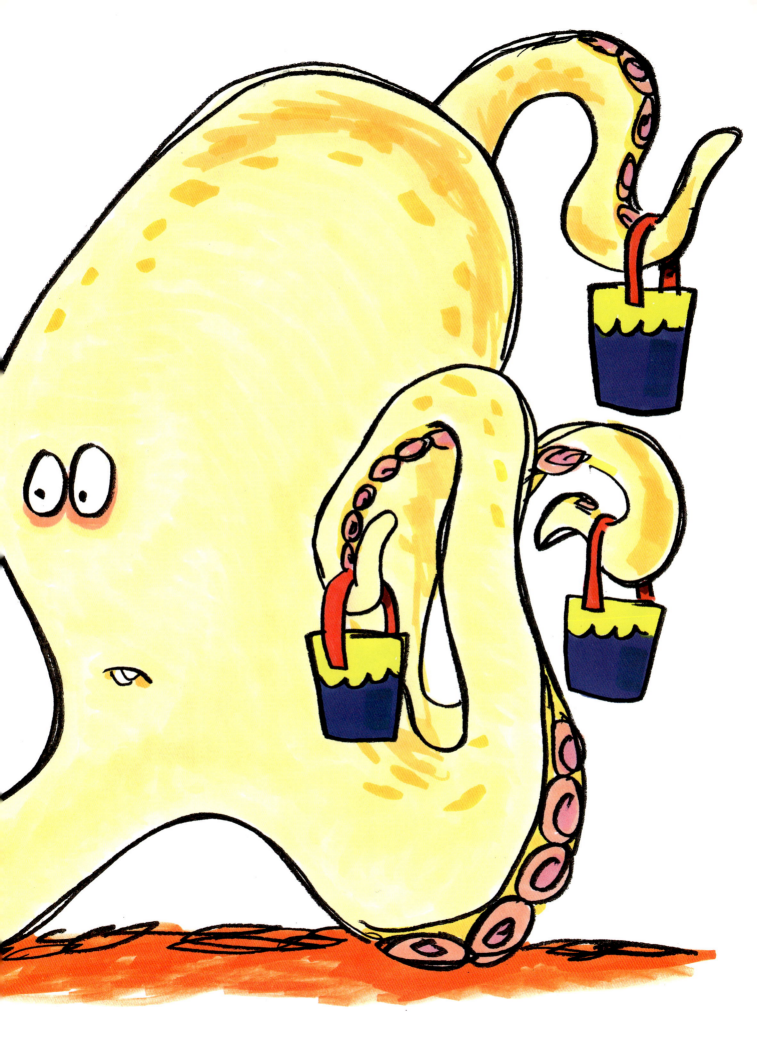

Is that BEAR all BARE?

BEAR: Large wild animal with shaggy hair, usually black or brown (don't feed them).

BARE: Without clothes or covering.

Does the HORSE sound HOARSE to you?

HORSE: Large four-legged animal used to carry riders and/or pull loads.

HOARSE: Having a sore or rough voice.

SALE: An exchange of goods or services for money.

SAIL: A trip or voyage on a boat or ship; a material used to catch the wind.

Has this **ONE**
WON
ONE or two?

ANT: Small insects that live in colonies.

AUNT: Sister of one's father or mother.

Did you see the FLEA FLEE?

FLEA: Tiny wingless jumping insect that lives on other animals.

FLEE: To run away or escape.

The **MAID** has **MADE** the bed.

MAID: Female house servant. **MADE:** Finished; completed; accomplished.

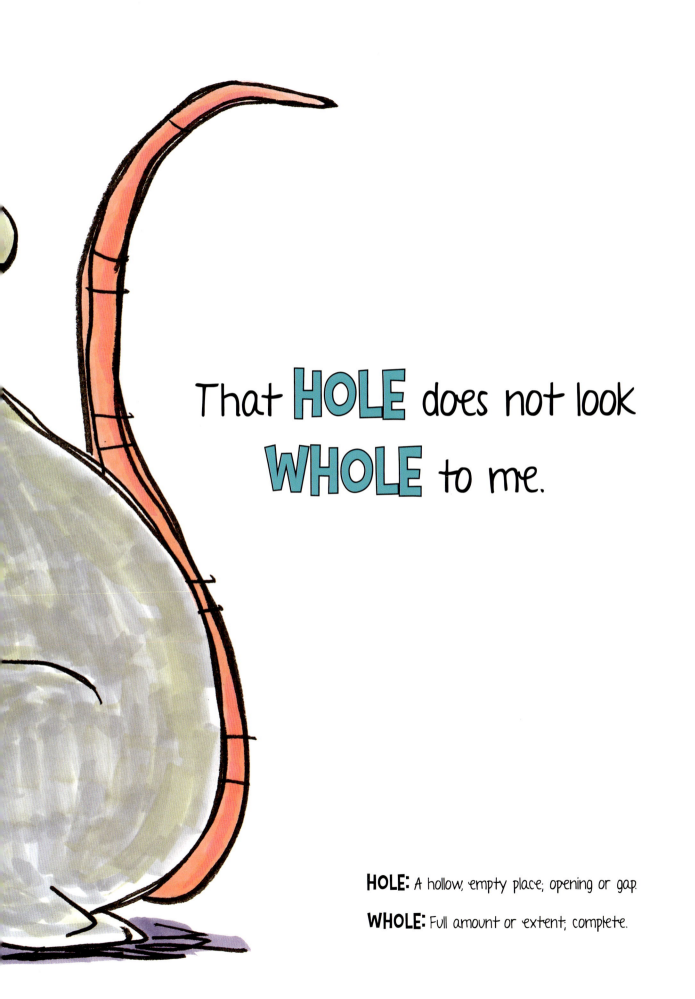

That **HOLE** does not look **WHOLE** to me.

HOLE: A hollow, empty place; opening or gap.

WHOLE: Full amount or extent; complete.

Have you **READ** what's **RED?**

READ: Past tense of reading.

RED: Color in rainbow with longest light wave; one of three primary colors.

Can you find a **PAIR** of **PEARS**?
Do you **HEAR** what's **HERE**?
These are more than just **MERE** words.
These are words that **MIRROR**.

MERE: Slight; simple; only.

MIRROR: A reflective glass.

But wait. Don't close the book.
It might look like you are done.

Turn the page. Read it again—
this time just for fun.

Can you find a **PAIR** of **PEARS?**

Do you **SEE** the **SEA?**

Would you like to **STARE** at **STAIRS?**

Or maybe **BE** a **BEE?**

Do you think the **DEER'S** a **DEAR?**

Is this **NOT** a **KNOT?**

Tell me what you **HEAR HERE.**

Last **NIGHT** the **KNIGHT** got caught.

Have you heard a **WHALE WAIL?**

Or seen a **HARE** with **HAIR?**

Do you think this **PAIL** is **PALE?**

Is that **BEAR** all **BARE?**

Does the **HORSE** sound **HOARSE** to you?

SALE or **SAIL**, you can't.

Has this **ONE WON ONE** or two?

Is that **ANT** an **AUNT?**

Did you see the **FLEA FLEE?**

The **MAID** has **MADE** the bed.

That **HOLE** does not look **WHOLE** to me.

Have you **READ** what's **RED?**

Can you find a **PAIR** of **PEARS?**

Do you **HEAR** what's **HERE?**

These are more than just **MERE** words.

These are words that **MIRROR.**

WORDS BY **M. AGRELIUS**

ILLUSTRATIONS BY **VAL CHADWICK BAGLEY**